Whispered Strengths

Amrutalakshmi VS

BookLeaf Publishing

India | USA | UK

To my Mother, Sujatha K,

and

my Aunt, Late. MG Pushpavalli

-     two strong women I have known.

Acknowledgement

To my love, my heart, my soul.
To God for blessing me and making me whole.
To my family, who stood by me through it all.
To the joy that lifted me and made me stand tall.
To the setbacks that gave me the strength to grow.
To the lessons that made my life glow.
To my friends, pillars of unwavering support.
To my publisher and team, who guided me throughout.
To my readers, for your love and cheer.

Preface

'I remembered that the real world was wide, and that a varied field of hopes and fears, of sensations and excitements, awaited those who had the courage to go forth into its expanse, to seek real knowledge of life amidst its perils'.
— **Charlotte Brontë, Jane Eyre**

From tender beginnings to growth, loss, love, dreams, hope, strength, and self-discovery, a woman's life is vibrant, challenging, and beautiful. This book explores their journey and diverse experiences, reflecting different phases of their lives. Dear readers, I invite you to walk alongside her and witness the moments of transformation and the everyday joys that define her path.

1. Hello World

Yet again, the earth bears witness,
A pure soul enters the world and joins many
others.
With tiny toes and cry so melodious,
An angel is born bearing invisible wings.

A beacon of love amid the gloom,
A ray of hope for the failing knot.
A purpose clear and hopes abloom,
Hearts beaming with endless delight.

Welcome, dear, to this marvellous world,
Of endless possibilities, of dreams.
With moist eyes, her parents behold,
Their love for her has no bounds.

Who is to tell what her future holds?
Very soon, her path will unfold.
Embracing the mystery, a blank canvas awaits,
To carve a fine story yet to be told.

2. Celebration Of A NewLife

The celebration begins to welcome the precious,
Laughter and joy fill the air.
She captures the hearts of everyone she meets
And gifts them with memories that are etched
forever.

Her first cry, her first smile,
Her first sneeze, her first sound,
Her first steps, her first fall,
Each milestone, every experience – profound.

With those curious eyes round and brown,
She watches in awe as the world goes by.
Boundless thirst for the known and unknown,
She explores everything, reaching for the sky.

She walks carefree and dances with grace,
With not a shadow of worry to slow her.
Laughter and talk brimming with innocence,
Makes you ache to be more like her.

3. Blooming

The earth awakens from her short rest,
Hues of green adorn every tree.
Tulips and daffodils in colours so bright,
Adds life to the world's rich tapestry.

Like this Spring that is in its prime,
She fills the air with joy and gleam.
Giggling like a bubbling stream,
She chases butterflies like a dream.

She wishes to become many things,
She goes to school and goes to play.
Brightening the world with her ways,
She makes friends, some forever to stay.

She pauses to enjoy the wonders all around,
Shut away from the endless race.
With a smile on her lips and feet on the ground,
She meets life with a beautiful grace.

4. Withered

Rain lashed at the rooftop, endlessly,
Casting a gloomy shadow all around her.
A myna cried in the distance helplessly,
Piercing the stillness of the damp air.

Her body burned from within, and she lay there,
Submitting herself to the rain's melancholy
power.
The more she wanted someone to hear,
The more she buried it deep under.

She looked in the mirror and stared into her eyes
Probing hard for a glimpse of her old self.
All she could feel was her heart, cold as ice,
Pressed against her chest, sans life.

She was robbed of her youth and innocence,
Her laughter became a distant memory.
She contemplated, but nothing made sense,
She longed for some light to set her free.

5. Hope

She keeps reiterating,
Another day, another chance.
She keeps waiting,
For new beginnings.

Pulling and pushing
When she moves forward.
There is always something
Forcing her to give ground.

Tug of war prevails,
Persistently between rational thinking
And puerile thoughts.
Endless struggle, unavailing.

Years are flying,
Today, indistinguishable from yesterday.
Only expectations lying,
Awaiting good tidings on the way.

6. Friends Forever

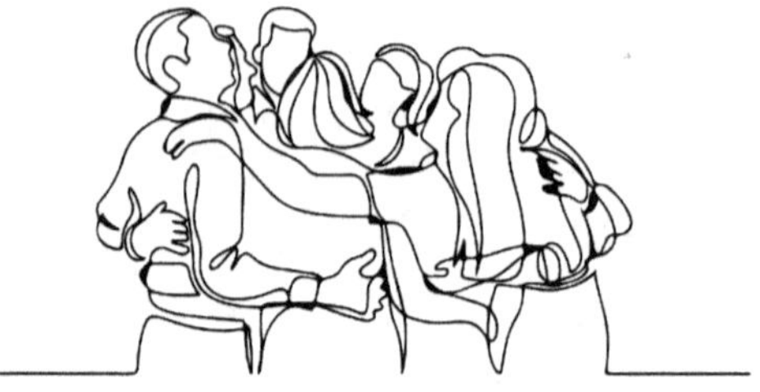

The world saw strength and resilience,
It was but a facade of happiness.
She dreams, works and strives,
But in her heart, a shadow persists.

She met them, a loyal clan,
Breaking through her darkest times.
Her pain and fear began to wane,
She learned to trust and to rise.

With them, time seemed to soar,
Her heart sprung with delight.
Their magic mended many a scar,
And eased her plight.

There is an oasis in the desert,
For every weary ship, there is a harbour.
A sanctuary where the wandering birds rest,
They became her haven, her armour.

7. Respite

Summer blazed, and the world surrendered,
Birds, thirsty and tired, yearned for a respite.
Every living being sought refuge in the shade,
Days stretched endlessly into the night.

Wells have dried up and the river runs thin,
Everyone mourns the loss of this divine source.
Yet when the monsoon hits again,
Her value is ignored, and we drift off course.

The heat and exhaustion did not bother her,
She ran around under the clear blue sky.
Open fields and high trees welcomed her.
Tan made her skin glow as bright as May.

For her, it was the happiest time,
Relishing the sweetness of juicy mangoes.
Playing with uncles, aunts and cousins,
Making lovely memories in abundance.

8. Her Muse

Cold moon, you rose high in glaring fury,
Not failing to surprise the town.
Burning the December night sky,
You put up a show for everyone.

It took a while, but slowly, your rage came down
Who was it that calmed your fuss?
Who was it that descended from heaven?
And caressed those dented contours.

Look at you now, blushing so bright,
You draw me towards you every night.
How beautiful you are, my muse, my light,
As the year ends, what a soothing sight.

You are the symbol of love and dreams,
Watching you every night wakes my heart.
Smiling and shining through the craters,
You reign the sky with all your might.

9. Endowed

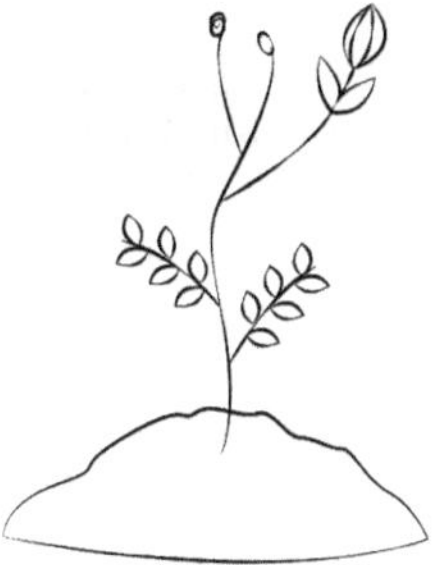

The weight of life pulls us down,
But with family's love, we'll find our way.
Though the world may twist and bend,
We hold on tight, come what may.

Mom and Dad, with minds so strong,
Blessed are those who have felt this grace.
Luckier are those who have a sibling,
A sibling's love, both bold and fierce.

So no matter the miles, no matter the time,
We are connected, always near.
Though far in the body, close in heart,
My sister, you are forever dear.

You see the world through different eyes,
I hold my views, and they are mine.
We both have different truths, different values,
Yet still, our hearts intertwine.

Our bond has grown with every passing year,
We are each other's strength and a steady guide.
Through all the storms and sky so clear,
There is nothing we cannot face, side by side.

10. New Beginnings

It was time to find her footing,
To shape her path anew.
To take that first step towards self-standing,
A turning point was in view.

A cumulation of all her choices,
And decisions led her here.
Amidst a swarm of people,
One is no different than the other.

Who to trust, who to doubt,
She's learned to tread with care throughout.
In no time, it was evident,
Many shared only a fleeting moment.

People come, and they go,
It was not about them anymore.
She went on to do what she had to,
And she did that like a pro.

11. Dear Pen

Dear pen, when I hold You to write,
I feel like clinging on to an old friend.
All my emotions come alive,
In every word, my heart, You mend.

You know my fears,
You know my strengths.
You know my tears,
You know my weaknesses.

Little devil, the feelings You squeeze out!
To my soul, You connect deep.
You understand me inside out,
You urge me to take that leap.

With each line, you trace my truth,
In Your presence, no secrets lie.
Together we travel through every depth,
With Your help, we soar, my thoughts and I.

12. Goodbye to A Friend

The sound of a horn echoed from a distance,
The train slowly moved on ahead,
Stealing from two friends,
Moments that were meant to be shared.

Her friend stood leaning by the door,
Tears streamed down warmly on their cheeks.
She saw the train disappear and stood there,
Her hands reached out to the empty space.

The place was noisy and packed to the rafters,
Suddenly, it seemed silent; time stood still.
A part of her gone, she stared blankly at the
tracks,
Throat choked and emotions invincible.

She wished life wouldn't pull them apart,
And create a void so vast.
Is this goodbye? She prayed not,
Her best friend, forever in her heart.

13. Changing Seasons

Autumn winds began to blow,
Leaves came floating down.
Red, rusty, gold and yellow,
Blanketed the roads like a vibrant gown.

Rain fell gently on the leaf bud,
Look at the wreath hung on every door.
The smell of pumpkin and the wet mud
Lingered in the frosty evening air.

Soon the trees turn barren and lifeless,
The ambience loses all its glow.
The earth turns cold and sleeps
Under layers and layers of snow.

The rhythm of carols fills the air,
Christmas lights bring about a radiant flare.
The world readies itself for a new year,
Embracing hope and a festive cheer.

14. Abode

Atop the mound in God's Own Country,
Welcoming her with all its beauty.
There is an abode so lovely,
Where she flees to, like a bird set free.

When the sun disappears down the hills,
Darkness spreads its cape over the place.
Nocturnal creatures raise their heads,
To watch thousands of fireflies dance.

Waking up rejuvenated to the birds singing,
She drinks her coffee, gazing at the hills.
Every day, she watches a bulbul come flying
And hopping around on the jackfruit trees.

Sitting on the verandah, she enjoys the rain,
Captivated by the scents and sounds.
Staring at the swaying coconut trees,
She savours these tranquil moments.

15. Mother

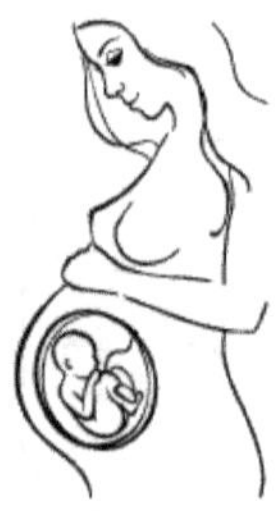

Ever since you entered this world,
She held you close to her.
You clung tight to her body, to her soul,
And she loved you like no other.

In a world that is boastful of its tiniest actions,
She quietly makes innumerable sacrifices.
She endures many sleepless nights,
She waves a tale in silent ways.

With an open heart, she stands by you,
Guides you through your ups and downs.
Her world revolves around you,
You find your role in her embrace.

Heart full of love, a mind so strong,
An inspiration for many a youth.
Even when her breath falters, she goes on,
Growing old with such grace and strength.

16. Random Thought

Look at the swarm of levered puppets,
Heads bent over fancy gizmos.
Shutting their eyes to the world outside,
Mind numbed to the rhythm outdoors.

Twilight paves the way for the young Moon,
Behold, the unceasing crowd jostling.
Cramped together and yet oceans apart,
cutting corners to grow, trudging.

Without a valiant fight for a purpose,
Are we to become one with the dust?
Like the cursed tides,
that do not touch the shores.

17. Finding Love

It was magic the day she saw him,
Her smile was so broad, her laugh was so open.
Like a moth to a flame, she ran to him,
She was happy like a child again.

She didn't know she could love again,
She dared to trust, dared to fall.
A love so unexpected and sudden,
She poured her soul and gave it all.

The feelings she had read of in books
She now felt firsthand, for real.
'Am I in a dream'? she wondered sometimes,
For everything seemed surreal.

Around him, her world revolved,
Soon enough, he was everything to her.
A shoulder to rest her weary head,
Someone to hold her hands forever.

18. Little Things

Waking up to a sunrise so beautiful,
Stars twinkling in a sky so clear,
The innocence of a baby's smile,
Joyful sights bring her cheer.

Mixed fragrances of flowers in bloom,
The scent of a newborn's head,
Petrichor rising from the damp earth's womb.
Little aromas that lift her mood.

Arms of a loved one wrapped so tight,
Fresh morning breeze kissing her forehead,
A baby's tiny fingers, soft and sweet,
Touches that bring comfort to her mind.

Hot coffee warming her mornings,
The lingering taste of mom's cuisine,
A shared meal with school friends,
Flavours she holds so close.

Laughter shared with friends so dear,
Rain softly drumming on the rooftop,
Waves caressing the sandy shore,
Soothing sounds that make her heart leap.

19. A Moment of Radiance

People moved to and fro across a bustling street,
I was moving with the crowd but came to a halt.
There, by the roadside, a small, fragile girl sat,
Staring at a distance, lost in some thought.

In a ragged gown, her spirit stood tall,
Her body was exposed to the changing seasons
of time.
She watched with longing a small girl,
Licking and relishing an ice cream.

I approached her gently, offering a treat,
She took the gift in her weak hands.
Her face lit up, and our gaze met.
She then ran away with a smile that reached her
eyes.

Like a parched land quenched by the first drop
of rainfall,
Her joy was profound and yet discreet.
Though I never saw her at all,
Her radiant eyes remain etched in my heart.

20. Coffee and Me

The world calmly and brightly awakens,
Through the curtains, the sun spills light softly.
I wake up to many thoughts,
A sweet one I cannot resist: Coffee!!

With a steaming cup in my hand, I embrace the
day,
Savouring the tranquillity of the early hours.
The world may rush, but for now, mine will stay,
As if to give a tender hug, the fragrant steam
rises.

When fragments of worry scatter in the mind,
Questions echo endlessly, and clarity fades.
Every sip pushes the chaos far behind,
And with a gentle sigh, my world restarts.

It's one of those joys that comforts deep,
In laughter, silence, joy and strife.
Like words from loved ones, I treasure and keep,
In many ways, this dreamy aroma has touched
my life.

21. Growing Old Gracefully

It took a lot of people and their drama,
Their pretence and boastful ways,
Innumerable downfalls, endless trauma,
To show her the path through the haze.

It's not the simplicity in the dress you wear,
But the thought that the world doesn't revolve
around you,
Piety and humbleness start from within,
From the wrong people, she learned it and grew.

The people you surround yourself,
It's amazing how they can shape your view,
When she realised that they were destroying her,
She shielded herself from toxicity, her strength anew.

Free from the worries that tomorrow might
bring,
All she needed was happiness and peace,
Free from the baggage of yesterday's sting,
She learned to love herself and grow old with
grace.